Elogio al disparate
Beatriz Santiago Muñoz
Secession

Ɛ
LOGIO
AL Ɗ
ISPARATE

Verlag der Buchhandlung Walther und Franz König, Köln

BEATRIZ SANTIAGO MUÑOZ AND CLAUDIA BECERRA IN CONVERSATION

5

6

Claudia,

I am sending you some ideas to start discussing the lack of sense, gibberish, and nonsensical poetry. Some points besides Clarice Lispector and the *caballo-yo*! I propose that we move in a free association mode, letting ourselves be carried away more by the ideas that cross our minds than by the desire to give form or meaning to what we write.

About the "caballo-yo"

During the weeks after the hurricane, when life was all about looking for food water gasoline electricity, I was standing in a kilometer-long line to get cash from an ATM when a man in his forties took two or three steps, half dizzy, towards the ATM, shouted "Yo soy un caballo!" (I am a horse!) and collapsed on the ground. The "caballo-yo"[1] *is then an idealized representation of the self. A very Caribbean idea... the "caballote" or "big horse" in Puerto Rico is a skilled, strong, capable man, an expert in his field, a respected man. I don't know to whom the prayer was addressed. Truth is, he wasn't looking at anyone in particular; it was at everyone, no one, or himself. There was no clear recipient. For that reason, it seemed to be addressed to a great other, not to us, who were just some random others lining up toward the machine that spits money. His voice said* I am a “caballote” *but his body collapsed like* a notwithstanding. *It has helped me understand a little more about the register of the real for Lacan.*

8

When I was little, my uncle Lonsi (Lonsi because his name was Miguel, like his father, and since his father was called Miguelón, he was Miguelonsito, which mutated to Lonsi) used to tell me: Lombriz Cien Fuego de la Hoz (describing Beatriz Santiago Muñoz).

The nonsense helps you understand from an early age that one word's meaning over another is an accident; it is arbitrary.

Remembering this made me think we should have several pseudonyms for this conversation. A pseudonym for each part of the conversation?

The pseudonym, hiding the name, or another name based on the first, inauguration of the proper name as a restriction or rhythm.

Francesc Tosquelles always said that having an accent, and being difficult to understand, was important for psychoanalytic treatment.

In fact, recently, some of us—you know who, the usual suspects—were talking about words used to name the female sex, which in my childhood were totally absent. The female sex was, not *missing, but in fact very present*, but it was not named. While for another person in their childhood, it may have had dozens of pseudonyms, but never vulva or vagina: little wallet, pocket, sheath. We think that, in this case, the proliferation of euphemisms also ends up indicating that it is unnameable or unmentionable.

In *La experiencia literaria* by Alfonso Reyes, he talks about jitanjáforas. Here, he talks about the word's origin in Mariano Brull's poem... there is a part that I love. Jehovah created the word. I can't find the year he wrote it but it's a great fable about language. Beautiful. Also, what he says about names...

I think about words-sounds, some already famous in Puerto Rico, like “ecuajey” or “equelequa”—and what happens when we all have a word that we share and that we enjoy but we don’t know exactly what it refers to—it’s an idea, a little ambiguous, it feels good in the mouth, it keeps transforming. “Equelequa” has something from Latin or French, which apparently means “that’s it.”

I know I took this photo in a museum in Isenheim while traveling through Alsace last year. But it reminded me that speaking in tongues is for madmen, the devil, or God. It is difficult to know if it is divine or satanic, a sign of genius or folly. This devil, I don’t know if it enters or leaves the mouth. It’s the same with the language that pierces us. I think that this painting is in the same museum as the Colmar triptych.

Hello Bea,

About names

Lombriz Cien Fuego de la Hoz would be a great pseudonym. During my brief stay at la iupi (University of Puerto Rico), one of my own was born, Severa Sarduy, a kind of tropical Fran Lebowitz... but like Fran, Severa has not yet produced much writing (haha). Let's see what names are born in the course of this conversation.

You remind me that I thought a lot about my name when I was a kid. My name is Claudia because of an aunt I never met. She, like another of my grandmother's daughters, died as a child from cystic fibrosis, an inherited condition that affects the lungs. It always seemed strange to me to respond to the name of a dead person.

In addition to the accident and the arbitrariness, I also think about what names designate and bequeath. Claudia comes from the Latin *claudus*, which means crippled. It is contained in the verb *claudicar*, or to give up.

This etymological dictionary has a theory about your name, and it seems that you are tied to the journey:

> *The word Beatriz possibly comes from the late Latin* Viatrix, *which in turn comes from* Viator *(traveler). Eventually, its spelling would be altered*

by association with beatus *(blessed, holy, happy) at the beginning of the Christian era. In fact, Simplicius, Faustino, and Beatrix were martyrs who died during the Diocletian persecution.*

I also think about that poem by Alejandra Pizarnik, *En esta noche en este mundo*:

no
las palabras
no hacen el amor
hacen la ausencia
si digo agua ¿beberé?
si digo pan ¿comeré?

no
words
do not make love
do not make absence
if I say water, will I drink?
if I say bread, will I eat?

I often read this poem alongside Saussure in my university classes to discuss arbitrariness and convention in language. The idea of not having a natural connection between words and things tortures Pizarnik. The poem is all in lowercase; it begins but never ends (it has no periods), and the commas are non-existent. Questions are marked. I am trying to say that Pizarnik describes a world without springs because even language does not contain what it names.

Water is a word that does not quench thirst. And worse still, does it produce it?

In Pizarnik, thirst is another word for dissatisfaction, lack, and desire.

Jitanjáforas. I have fond memories of that essay. I was still a college student when I read it and didn't understand much. Years later, while reading a collection of poems by Matos Paoli, *Variaciones del mar,* I thought again about the color "verdehalago" or "flattering-green" that Alfonso Reyes talks about at some point in the essay.

About Matos Paoli, it was a very crazy reading experience because I remember that there was such a precise and technical use of vocabulary related to the sea. At the same time, the poems were full of made-up words. In many cases, the great thing was not being able to identify the difference between the real words and the invented ones. The invented ones seemed real, and the real ones seemed invented. There was speculation, and in the end, the difference was irrelevant. In both cases, something was named that clearly existed in the world. Only the name was lacking.

I read it now and think about what happens with the words *racha* and *aguaje*. They have such specific meanings in our slang, but here, they appear in the context of poems that try to capture that great mythological object in constant transformation: the SEA. What happens to language in proximity to the sea? The sea makes language loosen up and do its thing. I think of Virginia Woolf's novel *The Waves* and of Martín Adán. When I read *racha* and *aguaje*, I feel that the slang (*mala racha*: bad luck; *aguaje*: lie) coexists with other meanings, perhaps more related to the lyrical. I didn't know that a *racha* is also a gust of wind. And *aguaje* has at least 15 definitions in the dictionary, eight of these linked to the sea. The result is the mix between the sacred and the sacrilegious? The sea does not cease like a bad streak. The image of the sea as a perpetual lie...

Hola Claudia,

About the childhood alias, something that has always been fundamental to my origin story, or rather questionable personal mythology, is that my parents did not give me a name or register me in the demographic registry until I was three. My father's letter to the registry is legendary, a false apology accompanied by a $1 money order to pay a fine for the delay. I have relied on that passive resistance to think of myself as a priori, free from destiny. I'm curious if the proper name as a blank space can function as a *point de capiton*, those places that weave the imaginary and the symbolic. Since I love the idea of emptiness and disorder, I also love the idea of not having a name—really.

I like what Julia Kristeva says about echolalias, invented words, musicality, and port-manteaus in this clip[2]. She relates it to the pre-oedipal, the maternal—and also the revolutionary.

When my son was about four or five years old and used to play with his older sister, if he wanted to change the rules of the game, if the little plastic Spiderman figure now had to represent the baker, he would ask his sister to repeat the word "baker" until he was satisfied with the change of identity. Then, the game would continue. At other times, he might need other adjustments, perhaps climatic: hail, hail, hail. I thought at that moment that language was like money, that it stays in circulation, that it keeps its value only through speaking—through repetition, building communal devotion. The more banal, the better stabilization of the word's value.

To a certain extent. Thinking of Pizarnik's poem, it may be the opposite: absence. Hail Hail Hail.

Now, at 17, the book he mostly returns to is *Poems and Antipoems* by Nicanor Parra. And when he comes home from school and wants to talk, the conversation invariably revolves around the rules of poetry, how free is free verse really, and the relationship between the aesthetic and the political.

On the other side, there is *disparate*[3]. Great word, vast possibilities, for instance in a mini-essay by José Carlos Mariátegui, *In defense of pure nonsense.*

> Pure nonsense certifies the death of the bourgeois absolute. It denounces the bankruptcy of a spirit, of a philosophy, more than a technique.
>
> —published in *Amauta,* N.º 13.
>
> Written by José Carlos Mariátegui, 1928

It gets to a similar place as the one Kristeva speaks of, nonsense as a revolutionary announcement and trace, the death of the bourgeois absolute. I love nonsense, but I no longer have illusions about death. I still attribute transformative capacities to nonsense, but the range is different.

Should we continue in the epistolary?

Hola Bea,

Sorry for the delay. Now, my paid job requires me to correct a lot of nonsense that I'm not really interested in correcting... I would also declare myself in defense of nonsense here, but they won't let me.

Your email brings me back to Martín Adán, with whom I had a brief obsession several years ago. When I went to Peru, I found the first edition of his *Diario de poeta* (A Poet's Diary). Nobody has that! Not even my Peruvian friends. Now the book is probably in one of the piles of books I still have in my apartment after moving.

I don't know which part of Adán's work Mariátegui refers to, but *Travesía de extramares* must be there. The strangeness of these poems lies in the mixture of tradition and avant-garde. This collection of poems was published in 1950 when the avant-garde had already passed its prime. Vallejo and Neruda had long ago published their monsters, *Trilce* and *Residencia en la tierra*.

Intentando poner en frases mi más oculta y sutil sensación —y desobedeciendo mi necesidad exigente de veracidad—, yo diría: si pudiese haber escogido, me habría gustado nacer caballo. Pero —quién sabe— quizás el caballo no sienta el gran símbolo de vida libre que nosotros sentimos en él. ¿Debo concluir entonces que el caballo sería sobre todo para ser sentido por mí? ¿El caballo representa la animalidad bella y suelta del ser humano? ¿Lo mejor del caballo el ser humano ya lo tiene? Entonces abdico de ser un caballo y con gloria paso a mi humanidad.

El caballo me indica lo que soy.

Clarice Lispector, Seco estudio de caballos, *1974; published in: Clarice Lispector,* Cuento, *Universidad Nacional Autónoma de México, Coordinación de Difusión Cultural Dirección De Literatura, Cuento Contemporáneo: 2011.*

Jehová se aburría divinamente.

—Me siento poeta — dijo al fin—. Sea la luz.

Y fue la luz. Y fueron creados tierra y cielos, las aves, los peces, los camellos, y el hombre. Adán recibió el encargo de denominar algunos entes secundarios de la creación; desde luego, los animales. Cuando acabó de nombrarlos todos, siguió a su vez creando objetos nuevos con la palabra. Y Jehová observó:

-Atajemos a Adán. De otra suerte, el mundo será pequeño para tanta creación y

el continente menor que el contenido, lo que significaría una peligrosa anticipación sobre mi lógica de extrema izquierda que, como lo mejor de mí mismo, dejo para el final.

Y como ya no se podía detener el ímpetu léxico de Adán, Jehová castigó algunas palabras, dejándolas como barcos vacios o señalándolas con la recelosa bandera negra. De aquí el ripio que no engendra, y el enigma que no concibe aunque vive hinchado de nada («lleno de todo lo que no es sustancia», hubiera dicho Gracián).

12 48 82

La palabra había alcanzado ya un temeroso atletismo cósmico. Su don de captación era en ocasiones absoluto. De aquí la magia en que la fórmula oral gobierna el fenómeno. De aquí el hermetismo: quien pose el nombre del dios posee al dios. Hay identidad entre el nombre y lo nombrado. Quien sepa mi nombre sustancial, ese dispondrá de mí a su antojo. Se explica el seudónimo; se explica la ocultación del patronímico en el que cae preso. Ivonne, Germaine, Georgette se resisten siempre a decirnos cómo las llaman en su pueblo y en la santa casa de su madre. El nombre de guerra permite el desliz subrepticio desde la familia hasta el teatro. El nombre de religión es la escapatoria del siglo. Luego conviene a la policía del universo que haya un límite, un momento en que la sobresaturación de energía haga estallar el fulminante de la palabra, un tabú que obligue a callar los vocablos demasiado potentes. Los términos sagrados no pueden enunciarse sin que sobrevengan catástrofes. No jurarás el nombre de Dios en vano. El verdadero nombre de Roma, el verdadero nombre de Alá son secretos, perdidos ya por la incuria de las generaciones, poseídos antes por escasos privilegiados que conocían los métodos de manejarlos sin peligro. El horror al nombre recóndito tiene raíces milenarias.

Alfonso Reyes, Las jitanjáforas, *1929, published on: www.cervantesvirtual.com/obra/la-experiencia-literaria-y-otros-ensayos (October 23, 2024).*

Mariano Brull, Verdehalago, Poemas en menguante, *1928, www.cervantesvirtual.com/obra/la-experiencia-literaria y otros-ensayos (October 23, 2024).*

VERDEHALAGO

Por el verde, verde
verdería de verde mar
erre con erre.

Viernes, vírgula, virgen
enano verde
verdularia cantárida
erre con erre.

Verdor y verdín
verdumbre y verdura.
Verde, doble verde
de col y lechuga.
Erre con erre
en mi verde limón
pájara verde.

Por el verde, verde
verdehalago húmedo
extiéndome. Extiéndete.
Vengo de Mundodolido
y en Verdehalago me estoy.

En esta noche, en este mundo

A Martha Isabel Moia

en esta noche en este mundo
las palabras del sueño de la infancia de la muerta
nunca es eso lo que uno quiere decir
la lengua natal castra
la lengua es un órgano de conocimiento
del fracaso de todo poema
castrado por su propia lengua
que es el órgano de la re-creación
del re-conocimiento
pero no el de la re-surrección
de algo a modo de negación
de mi horizonte de maldoror con su perro
y nada es promesa
entre lo decible
que equivale a mentir
(todo lo que se puede decir es mentira)
el resto es silencio
sólo que el silencio no existe

no
las palabras
no hacen el amor
hacen la ausencia
si digo agua ¿beberé?
si digo pan ¿comeré?
en esta noche en este mundo
extraordinario silencio el de esta noche
lo que pasa con el alma es que no se ve
lo que pasa con la mente es que no se ve
lo que pasa con el espíritu es que no se ve

¿de dónde viene esta conspiración de invisibilidades?
ninguna palabra es visible

Alejandra Pizarnik, En esta noche, en este mundo, *1972: published in: Alejandra Pizarnik,* Textos de sombra y últimos poemas, *1971–1972, Editorial Sudamericana: 1982.*

53

Racha, Furia
De continuidad.
El mar no cesa nunca.
Diamante tras diamante nos subleva.
El fondo, siempre nuevo,
En la planicie que se vuelca azul.
Sangre que se derrama y se recoge.
A veces pálida
Como la muerte subitánea.
A veces floración de orilla a orilla.
El palmar, centinela.
En su oscuro ramaje permanece
Este aguaje perpetuo que retrata la apariencia en su
nimbo delator.

Francisco Matos Paoli, Variaciones del mar,
published in: Ediciones Juan Ponce de León, San Juan,
Puerto Rico: 1973.

24 60 94

TRILCE LXXVII DE CÉSAR VALLEJO

Graniza tanto, como para que yo recuerde
y acreciente las perlas
que he recogido del hocico mismo
de cada tempestad.

No se vaya a secar esta lluvia.
A menos que me fuese dado
caer ahora para ella, o que me enterrasen
mojado en el agua
que surtiera de todos los fuegos.

¿Hasta dónde me alcanzará esta lluvia?
Temo me quede con algún flanco seco;
temo que ella se vaya, sin haberme probado
en las sequías de increíbles cuerdas vocales,
por las que,
para dar armonía,
hay siempre que subir ¡nunca bajar!
¿No subimos acaso para abajo?

¡Canta, lluvia, en la costa aún sin mar!

César Vallejo, Trilce, *1922*

El disparate puro certifica la defunción del absoluto burgués. Denuncia la quiebra de un espíritu, de una filosofía, más que una técnica.

José Carlos Mariátegui, Defensa del disparate puro, *1928, published in: Sociedad Editora* Amauta, *N°13, Lima: 1928, p. 11.*

VOLTA SUBITO

¡Oh muerte que das vida!
Fray Luis de León

Now more than ever seems it rich to die
Keats

—¡Compás de la Bogada de Caronte,
Tú libérame ya de sutileza,
Madre y caudal de lágrima que empieza
En mí y no para ni en el horizonte!
—¡Dame tu ceguedad con qué yo afronte
Rumbo infinible de vida y belleza!...
¡Y la mudez con que el eterno expresa!...
¡Y el mi cadáver la tu boza apronte!
—¡Más no discurra yo sobre la linfa,
Ni rebusque ni finja, en haz o seno
De insondable hora, nenúfar o ninfa!
—¡De los ojos del muerto, mi mirada
Paire en faceta a luz cristalizada
Y yo mire belleza así sereno!

Martín Adán, Volta subito, *1939; published in* La rosa de la espinela: Martín Adán, *Selección y nota de SERGIO MONSALVO, 2012, Universidad Nacional Autonóma de México, Coodinación de Difusión Cultural, Dirección de Literatura: 2012, pp.10, 11; www.materialdelectura.unam.mx/poesia-moderna/16-poesia-moderna-cat/279-129-martin-adan (October 23, 2024).*

El incomprendido, *original lyric by Bobby Capó,*
transcription of the version sung by Ismael Rivera on the album
EL INCOMPRENDIDO, *Fania Records 1972.*

36 72 106

Por eso sé que solo voy
Yo no fui nada, nada, nada soy
Bituqui, baquilinbin para ti, pero que yo, yo, yo, yo, yo,
yo solo estaré
Y juraré que cuando muera
Belén, que aun así con mis presagios
pondré tu nombre a flor de labios y moriré
incomprendido
Yo soy Maelo, el incomprendido

This booklet is a supplement to the publication Elogio al disparate *by Beatriz Santiago Muñoz at Secession, Vienna 2024.*

Who knows why Adán chose to publish a book of sonnets in the fifties, full of epigraphs (something like Benjamin's *Arcades Project*)? The book is one of Adán's least known, probably because it is the closest to nonsense. The poems are very complicated to read because the words strung together one after another hardly produce meaning. Also, the sounds, the verse breaks, and the rhythms are uncomfortable; they generate a lot of dissonance. But thinking about this, aside from the fact that Adán wrote these sonnets in front of a Peruvian coast listening to Chopin's *Nocturnes*, says a lot, although I don't know exactly what. He doesn't abandon tradition but makes it so strange that he turns it into noise and nonsense.

I think he has many similarities with Matos Paoli, actually.

Here are some poems in case you want to not understand, but listen, for a while.[4]

Let's continue our epistlessss,
Claudia

Claudia,
Thanks for sending Martín Adan.

I will stick with this poem because of the Charon's rowing that it mentions, to not-understand why I was stuck a few weeks ago on that other one that invokes Charon with its "twice victorious I crossed the Acheron"—and which I only know through Kristeva! The last poem written by Nerval, *El desdichado* (you just texted me that it reminds you of *El incomprendido* by Maelo![5]) before he committed suicide, I think, after the death of his beloved. Kristeva builds much of *Black Sun,* her book on melancholy, from this poem.

The new words—infinible?—and that *Paire in facet*, are we in “a pair”?

Translated from Spanish by
Nicole C. Delgado Poueymirou

38

1 We chose to keep the Spanish original "*caballo-yo*," which roughly translate to "horse-I," to keep in mind the interplay with the sound of the words, and the idea of a "yo-yo" embedded in it.

2 www.youtube.com/watch?v=tNkLlxzZTys (November 19, 2024)

3 *Disparate* in Spanish, with no literal translation, refers to the act of talking nonsense or incorrectly.

4 www.materialdelectura.unam.mx/poesia-moderna/16-poesia-moderna-cat/279-129-martin-adan?start=3 (November 19, 2024)

5 Maelo was the nickname of Ismael Rivera (1931–1987), a Puerto Rican Salsa singer.

40

BEATRIZ SANTIAGO MUÑOZ Y CLAUDIA BECERRA EN CONVERSACIÓN

42

Claudia,

Aquí te envío algunas ideas para comenzar a hablar del no-sentido y de la jitanjáfora. Algunos puntos además de Clarice Lispector y el caballo-yo! Propongo que nos movamos a modo de libre asociación, dejándonos llevar más por las ideas que se nos cruzan que por el deseo de darle forma o sentido a lo que escribimos.

> *Sobre el caballo-yo*
>
> *Durante las semanas después del huracán, durante las cuales la vida entera era buscar comida agua gasolina y electricidad, estaba parada en una fila kilométrica para sacar efectivo de un cajero automático cuando un hombre de unos cuarentaypico de años dio dos o tres pasos medio mareado hacia el cajero, gritó "Yo soy un caballo!" y colapsó en el suelo. El caballo-yo es entonces una representación idealizada del yo. Muy caribeña la idea…el caballote en Puerto Rico es un hombre hábil, fuerte, capaz, un duro en su ámbito, de respetar. No sé a quién estaba dirigida la plegaria. La verdad es que él no miraba a nadie en específico, era a todos y nadie, o a él mismo. No había destinatario claro. Por eso mismo parecía*

estar dirigida a un gran otro, no a nosotros, que sólo éramos unos otromáses enfilados hacia la máquina que escupe dinero. Su voz decía Yo soy un caballote, *pero su cuerpo colapsaba como un* no obstante. *Me ha ayudado a entender un poco más eso del registro de lo real para Lacan.*

44

Cuando era pequeña, mi tío Lonsi (Lonsi porque su nombre era Miguel, igual que su papá, y como a su papá le decían Miguelón, entonces él era Miguelonsito, que mutó a Lonsi) me decía: Lombriz Cien Fuego de la Hoz (por Beatriz Santiago Muñoz).

El disparate te ayuda a entender desde temprano que el sentido que tiene una palabra sobre otra es un accidente, es arbitrario.

Recordar esto me hizo pensar en que deberíamos tener varios pseudónimos para esta conversación. ¿Un pseudónimo para cada parte de la conversación?
El pseudónimo, ocultar el nombre. O otro nombre basado en el primer nombre, inauguración del nombre propio como restricción o ritmo.
Francesc Tosquelles siempre decía que tener un acento, ser difícil de entender, era importante para la cura psicoanalítica.

De hecho, recientemente estábamos hablando algunos—ya tu sabes quiénes, los de siempre—sobre las palabras para el sexo femenino, que en mi niñez estuvieron totalmente ausentes, el sexo femenino estaba, no es que *estuviese desaparecido, de hecho estaba muy presente*, pero no se nombraba. Mientras que para otra persona en su infancia tenía decenas de pseudónimos, pero nunca vulva o vagina: carterita, bolsillo, vaina. Pensamos que en este caso la proliferación de eufemismos también acaba por indicar que es innombrable o inmencionable.

En *La experiencia literaria*, Alfonso Reyes habla sobre las jitanjáforas. Aquí, habla del origen de la palabra en el poema de Mariano Brull... Hay una parte que me encanta. Jehová creó la palabra. No encuentro el año en que lo escribió, pero es una gran fábula sobre el lenguaje. Hermoso. También lo que dice sobre los nombres...

Pienso en palabras-sonidos ya famosas en Puerto Rico, como “ecuajey” o “equelequá”, y en eso que sucede cuando tenemos todos una palabra compartida y que disfrutamos pero que no sabemos exactamente a qué se refiere—es una idea, un poco ambigua, se siente bien en la boca, se va transformando. El equelequá tiene algo de latín o francés y parece significar “he ahí la cosa”.

Sé que tomé esta foto en un museo en Isenheim, cuando viajaba el año antepasado por Alsacia. Pero me recordó que hablar en lenguas es de locos, del diablo o de dios. Es difícil saber si es divino o satánico, una señal de genio o de imbecilidad. Ese demonio, no sé bien si entra o sale de la boca. Pasa igual con el lenguaje que nos atraviesa. Esta pintura me parece que está en el mismo museo en donde se encuentra el tríptico de Colmar.

Hola Bea,

Sobre los nombres

Lombriz Cien Fuego de la Hoz sería tremendo pseudónimo. En mi breve estadía en la iupi (Universidad de Puerto Rico) nació uno mío, Severa Sarduy, una especie de Fran Lebowitz tropical... pero igual que Fran, Severa aún no produce mucha escritura (jaja). A ver qué nombres nacen en el curso de esta conversación.

Me recuerdas que de chamaca pensaba mucho en mi nombre. Me llamo Claudia porque una tía que nunca conocí se llamaba Claudia. Ella, igual que otra hija de mi abuela, murió de niña por fibrosis quística, una condición que se hereda y afecta los pulmones. Siempre me pareció raro responder al nombre de una muerta.

Además del accidente y la arbitrariedad, también pienso en lo que designan y legan los nombres. Claudia viene del latín *claudus,* que significa cojo. Está contenido en el verbo *claudicar.*

Este diccionario etimológico tiene una teoría sobre tu nombre y parece que estás atada al viaje:

> *La palabra Beatriz posiblemente proviene del latín tardío* Viatrix, *que a su vez viene de* Viator *(viajero). Eventualmente, su grafía se alteraría*

por asociación con beatus *(beato, bendito, feliz), en los inicios de la era cristiana. De hecho Simplicius, Faustino y Beatrix fueron mártires que murieron durante la persecución de Dioclediano.*

También pienso en ese poema de Alejandra Pizarnik, *En esta noche en este mundo*:

no
las palabras
no hacen el amor
hacen la ausencia
si digo agua ¿beberé?
si digo pan ¿comeré?

Suelo leer ese poema de lado a Saussure en mis clases en la universidad para hablar de arbitrariedad y convención en el lenguaje. La idea de que no hay un nexo natural entre las palabras y las cosas produce monstruos en Pizarnik. El poema está todo en minúsculas, empieza pero nunca termina (no hay puntos), y las comas, inexistentes. Las preguntas sí se marcan. Lo que estoy tratando de decir es que Pizarnik describe un mundo sin resortes porque ni el lenguaje contiene lo que nombra.

Agua es una palabra que no sacia la sed. Y peor aún, ¿la produce?

En Pizarnik, sed es otra palabra para insatisfacción, falta, deseo.

56

Las jitanjáforas. Tengo un bonito recuerdo de ese ensayo. Yo era todavía estudiante de bachillerato cuando lo leí y no entendía mucho. Años después, mientras leía un poemario de Matos Paoli, *Variaciones del mar*, volví a pensar en el color verdehalago del que habla Alfonso Reyes en algún momento del ensayo.

Sobre Matos Paoli, fue una experiencia de lectura bien loca porque recuerdo que había un manejo tan preciso y técnico del vocabulario referente al mar, a la vez que los poemas estaban llenos de palabras inventadas. Lo genial era en muchos casos no poder identificar la diferencia entre las reales y las inventadas. Las inventadas parecían reales y las reales, inventadas. Se especulaba y al final la diferencia daba lo mismo. En ambos casos se nombraba algo que claramente existía en el mundo. Sólo faltaba el nombre.

Y ahora que lo leo pienso en lo que ocurre con las palabras racha y aguaje. Tienen significados tan específicos en nuestra jerga, pero aquí aparecen en el contexto de poemas que intentan capturar a ese gran objeto mitológico en constante transformación: ¿el/la? MAR. ¿Qué le ocurre al lenguaje en proximidad al mar? El mar hace que el lenguaje se afloje y haga lo suyo. Pienso en la novela *The Waves* de Virginia Woolf y en Martín Adán. Cuando leo racha y aguaje siento que la jerga (mala racha: mala suerte; aguaje: mentira) coexiste con otros significados quizás más asociados a lo lírico. No sabía que una racha también es una ráfaga de viento. Y aguaje tiene al menos 15 definiciones de el diccionario, ocho de éstas vinculadas al mar. ¿El producto es la mezcla entre lo sagrado y lo sacrílego? El mar no cesa, como una mala racha. La imagen del mar como un embuste perpetuo...

Hola Claudia,

En relación al alias infantil, algo que siempre ha sido fundamental en mi historia de origen, o más bien mi cuestionable mitología personal, es que mis papás no me pusieron nombre ni me inscribieron en el registro demográfico hasta los 3 años. La carta de mi papá al registro es legendaria, una falsa disculpa acompañada por la multa de $1 en giro postal por la tardanza. Me he apoyado sobre esa resistencia pasiva para pensarme a priori libre de destino. Me pregunto si el nombre propio como lugar en blanco puede funcionar como un *point de capiton,* esos lugares en donde se teje lo imaginario y lo simbólico. Como estoy enamorada de la idea del vacío y del desorden, me encanta la idea de no tener nombre—realmente.

Me gusta lo que dice Julia Kristeva en este clip[1] sobre las ecolalias, las palabras inventadas, la musicalidad y los port-manteaus. Lo relaciona a lo pre-edipal, a lo maternal—y también a lo revolucionario.

Cuando mi hijo tenía unos cuatro ó cinco años y jugaba con su hermana mayor, si quería que las condiciones del juego cambiaran, si la figurita plástica del hombre araña ahora debía representar al panadero, él le pedía a su hermana que repitiera la palabra "panadero" hasta que se sintiera satisfecho del cambio de identidad. Después, el juego continuaba. En otros momentos, habría que hacer otros ajustes, quizás climáticos: granizo, granizo, granizo.

Pensé en aquel momento que el lenguaje era como el dinero, que se mantiene en circulación, que mantiene su valor sólo mediante el hablar: mediante la repetición, construyendo devoción comunal. Mientras más banal, mejor estabilización del valor de la palabra.

Hasta cierto punto. Pensando en el poema de Pizarnik, puede ser lo opuesto, la ausencia. Granizo Granizo Granizo.

Ahora, a sus 17 años, su libro más manoseado es *Poemas y antipoemas* de Nicanor Parra. Y cuando llega de la escuela y quiere hablar, la conversación invariablemente gira alrededor de las reglas de la poesía, de qué tan libre es el verso libre y de la relación entre lo estético y político. Del otro lado, se encuentra el disparate. Gran palabra, amplias posibilidades, por ejemplo en un mini-ensayo de José Carlos Mariátegui, *En defensa del disparate puro.*

> El disparate puro certifica la defunción del absoluto burgués. Denuncia la quiebra de un espíritu, de una filosofía, más que una técnica.
>
> (Publicado en *Amauta*, N.º 13.
> Escrito por José Carlos Mariátegui, 1928)

Llega a un lugar similar que el que habla Kristeva,

el disparate como anuncio y trazo revolucionario, defunción del absoluto burgués. Amo el disparate pero ya no tengo ilusiones sobre defunciones. Le sigo atribuyendo capacidades transformadoras al disparate, pero son de otro registro.

¿Seguimos epistolares?

Hola Bea,

Perdona la demora. Ahora mi trabajo remunerado exige que corrija mucho disparate que realmente no me interesa corregir... Me declararía también en defensa del disparate aquí, pero no me dejan.

Tu correo me devuelve a Martín Adán, con quien tuve una breve obsesión hace varios años. Cuando fui a Perú encontré una primera edición de su *Diario de poeta*. ¡Nadie tiene eso! Ni mis amigos peruanos. Ahora el libro está en alguna de las montañas de libros que tengo en el piso todavía post-mudanza.

No sé a cuál parte del trabajo de Adán se refiere Mariátegui, pero *Travesía de extramares* debe estar ahí. La extrañeza de estos poemas radica en la mezcla entre tradición y vanguardia. Ese poemario fue publicado para 1950, cuando ya las vanguardias habían pasado por su mejor momento. Vallejo y Neruda habían publicado sus monstruos, *Trilce* y *Residencia en la tierra*, hacía ya mucho.

Por qué Adán, hacia los 50, decide publicar un libro de sonetos, lleno de epígrafes (algo así como el *Arcades Project* de Benjamin), quién sabe. El libro es de los menos conocidos de Adán, probablemente porque es el más cercano al disparate. Los poemas son muy complicados de leer porque las palabras hiladas una detrás de otra difícilmente generan sentido. Además, los sonidos, los cortes de verso, los ritmos, son incómodos, generan muchas disonancias. Pero pensar en esto, de lado a que Adán escribió estos sonetos frente a una costa peruana escuchando los *Nocturnos* de Chopin dice mucho, aunque no sé exactamente qué. No abandona la tradición pero la vuelve extraña hasta que la relocaliza en el ruido y el disparate.

Creo que tiene muchos parecidos con Matos Paoli, de hecho.

Acá hay algunos poemas, por si quieres no entender, pero escuchar, un rato.[2]

Seguimos nuestras epístolassss,
Claudia

Claudia,

Gracias por el envío de Martín Adan.

Me quedo en este poema por la bogada de Caronte que menciona, para no-entender, porque se me quedó atravesado hace unas semanas ese otro que invoca a Caronte con su "dos veces victorioso crucé el Aqueronte", ¡y al cual conozco sólo a través de Kristeva! El último poema de Nerval, *El desdichado* (¡me acabas de decir por texto que te recuerda a *El incomprendido* de Maelo![3]), me parece, antes de suicidarse, después de la muerte de su amada. Kristeva construye mucho del *Sol de Medianoche*, su libro sobre la melancolía, desde este poema.

Las nuevas palabras—¿infinible?—y ese *Paire en faceta*, ¿estaremos en "un par"?

1 www.youtube.com/watch?v=tNkLlxzZTys (19. noviembre de 2024)

2 www.materialdelectura.unam.mx/poesia-moderna/16-poesia-moderna-cat/279-129-martin-adan?start=3 (19. noviembre de 2024)

3 Maelo era el apodo de Ismael Rivera (1931–1987), cantante de salsa puertorriqueño.

74

BEATRIZ SANTIAGO MUÑOZ UND CLAUDIA BECERRA IM GESPRÄCH

75

76

Claudia,

ich schicke Dir hier einige Ideen, damit wir anfangen, über den Nichtsinn und die *jitanjáfora*[1] zu sprechen. Außerdem einige Punkte zu Clarice Lispector und dem Pferde-Ich! Ich schlage vor, dass wir im Sinne der freien Assoziation vorgehen, sodass wir uns treiben lassen von den Ideen, die uns in den Sinn kommen, anstatt vom Wunsch, dem, was wir schreiben, Form oder Sinn zu verleihen.

Über das Pferde-Ich

Während der Wochen nach dem Hurrikan, in denen das Leben daraus bestand, Essen, Wasser, Benzin und Strom zu finden, wartete ich in einer kilometerlangen Schlange, um Bargeld von einem Bankomaten abzuheben, als ein Mann etwas über vierzig halb benommen zwei oder drei Schritte Richtung Bankomat machte und schrie: „Ich bin ein Pferd!", und ohnmächtig zu Boden fiel. Das Pferde-Ich ist also eine idealisierte Repräsentation des Ichs. Ziemlich karibisch, diese Idee … in Puerto Rico ist der caballote *ein geschickter, starker, fähiger Mann, ein harter Kerl auf seinem Gebiet, einer, den man respektiert. Ich weiß nicht, an wen das Gebet gerichtet war.*

In Wahrheit sah er niemanden Bestimmten an, es galt allen oder keinem oder ihm selbst. Es gab natürlich keinen Empfänger. Genau deshalb schien es so, als gälte es einem höheren Etwas, nicht uns, den in der Schlange auf den Geld spuckenden Automaten Wartenden. Seine Stimme sagte: „Ich bin ein caballote*", aber sein Körper kollabierte dennoch. Das hat mir geholfen, das Register des Realen von Lacan besser zu verstehen.*

78

Als ich klein war, sagte mein Onkel Lonsi (Lonsi weil sein Name Miguel war, genauso wie der seines Vaters, welchen sie Miguelón nannten, daher war er Miguelonsito, was schließlich zu Lonsi führte) zu mir: Lombriz Cien Fuego de la Hoz (von Beatriz Santiago Muñoz).

Der Unsinn hilft dir schon früh zu verstehen, dass die Bedeutung, die ein Wort über das andere hat, purer Zufall ist, es ist Willkür.

Diese Erinnerung ließ mich daran denken, dass wir für diese Konversation verschiedene Pseudonyme haben sollten. Ein Pseudonym für jeden Teil dieser Konversation? Das Pseudonym, den Namen verbergen. Oder ein anderer Name, der auf dem Vornamen beruht, die Einführung des Eigennamens als Einschränkung oder Rhythmus.

Francesc Tosquelles sagte stets, dass einen Akzent zu haben, schwer zu verstehen zu sein, wichtig für die psychoanalytische Heilung sei.

Tatsächlich redeten wir vor Kurzem – du weißt schon wer, die Üblichen – über die Bezeichnungen für das weibliche Geschlecht, die in meiner Kindheit vollkommen abwesend waren, das weibliche Geschlecht gab es, es ist nicht so, *als wäre dieses verschollen, tatsächlich war es sogar sehr präsent*, aber man hat es nicht benannt. Für andere Personen gab es in der Kindheit Dutzende von Pseudonymen dafür, aber nie Vulva oder Vagina: Tasche,

Geldbörse oder Hülse. Wir dachten, dass in diesem Fall die Verbreitung von Euphemismen auch dazu diente, darauf hinzuweisen, dass etwas unnennbar oder nicht erwähnbar ist.

In seinem Werk *La experiencia literaria* spricht Alfonso Reyes über *jitanjáfora*. Da beschreibt er den Ursprung des Wortes im Gedicht von Mariano Brull … es gibt eine Stelle, die ich sehr mag. Jehova erschuf das Wort. Ich kann das Jahr nicht finden, in welchem er es schrieb, aber es ist eine tolle Fabel über die Sprache. Einfach wundervoll. Auch, was er über Namen sagt …

Ich denke an Wort-Klänge, bekannt in Puerto Rico, wie „ecuajey“ oder „equelequa“ – und das, was passiert, wenn wir alle ein gemeinsames Wort haben und es genießen, dieses zu verwenden, aber eigentlich nicht genau wissen, was es bedeutet – es ist eine Idee, ein bisschen ambivalent, die sich gut auf der Zunge anfühlt und sich laufend verändert. „Equelequa“ kommt wohl aus dem Lateinischen oder Französischen und scheint zu bedeuten: So ist es.

Ich weiß, dass ich dieses Foto in einem Museum in Isenheim gemacht habe, als ich vorletztes Jahr im Elsass herumgereist bin. Aber es erinnerte mich daran, dass in Zungen zu reden entweder verrückt/teuflisch oder göttlich ist. Es ist schwer zu wissen, ob etwas von göttlicher oder teuflischer Natur ist, ein Zeichen von Genialität oder Schwachsinn. Dieser Teufel, ich weiß nicht genau, ob er erst in dem Mund oder aus dem Mund kommt. Genauso ist es mit der Sprache, die uns durchquert. Mir kommt vor, dass dieses Gemälde im selben Museum ist wie das Triptychon von Colmar.

Hallo Bea,

zu den Namen:

Lombriz Cien Fuego de la Hoz wäre ein großartiges Pseudonym. Während meines kurzen Aufenthalts an der IUPI (Universität von Puerto Rico) entstand eines meiner eigenen Pseudonyme, Severa Sarduy, eine Art tropischer Fran Lebowitz … aber genauso wie Fran schreibt Severa noch immer nicht sonderlich viel (haha). Mal sehen, welche Namen noch während dieser Konversation entstehen.

Du erinnerst mich daran, dass ich als junges Mädchen sehr oft über meinen Namen nachgedacht habe. Ich heiße Claudia, weil eine Tante, die ich nie kennengelernt habe, Claudia hieß. Sie, auch eine weitere Tochter meiner Großmutter, starb als Kind an zystischer Fibrose, einer vererbbaren Erkrankung, welche die Lunge schädigt. Es kam mir schon immer komisch vor, auf den Namen einer Toten zu hören.

Über die Zufälligkeit und Willkür hinaus, denke ich auch darüber nach, was Namen bestimmen und hinterlassen. Claudia kommt aus dem Lateinischen, *claudus*, und heißt so viel wie lahm, enthalten im Verb *claudicar* (aufgeben).

Dieses etymologische Wörterbuch beinhaltet eine Theorie über Deinen Namen, und es scheint so, als ob du sehr dem Reisen zugeneigt wärst.

Das Wort Beatriz stammt wahrscheinlich aus dem Spätlateinischen, Viatrix, das wiederum von Viator (Reisender) kommt. Schließlich passte man die Schreibweise zu Beginn des christlichen Zeitalters an beatus an (gesegnet, heilig, glücklich). Tatsächlich waren Simplicius, Faustinus und Beatrix Märtyrer, die durch Diokletians Verfolgung den Tod fanden.

Ich denke auch an dieses Gedicht von Alejandra Pizarnik, *En esta noche en este mundo* („In dieser Nacht in dieser Welt"):

no
las palabras
no hacen el amor
hacen la ausencia
si digo agua ¿beberé?
si digo pan ¿comeré?

nein
die wörter
machen keine liebe
sie machen abwesenheit
wenn ich wasser sage trinke ich?
wenn ich brot sage esse ich?

Ich lese dieses an Saussure angelehnte Gedicht oft in meinen Vorlesungen an der Uni, um über die Willkürlichkeit und die Konvention in der Sprache zu sprechen. Die Idee, dass es keine natürliche Verbindung zwischen Wörtern und Dingen gibt, erschafft bei Pizarnik Ungeheuer. Das Gedicht besteht vollkommen aus Kleinbuchstaben, es fängt an, hört jedoch nie auf (es gibt keine Punkte), und die Beistriche sind inexistent. Die Fragen sind sehr wohl als solche gekennzeichnet. Das, was ich hiermit aufzeigen will, ist, dass Pizarnik eine Welt ohne Triebfeder beschreibt, weil nicht einmal die Sprache das beinhaltet, was sie benennt.

Wasser ist ein Wort, das den Durst nicht stillt. Und schlimmer noch, das den Durst erst auslöst?

Bei Pizarnik ist Durst ein anderes Wort für Unzufriedenheit, Mangel, Verlangen.

Die *jitanjáforas.* Ich habe eine schöne Erinnerung an diesen Essay. Ich war noch Schülerin der Oberstufe, als ich ihn las, und ich verstand damals nicht viel. Jahre später, als ich eine Gedichtsammlung von Matos Paoli las, *Variaciones del mar*, musste ich wieder an die grün-halagisch Farbe denken, von der Alfonso Reyes an einer bestimmten Stelle spricht.

Zu Matos Paoli: Es war eine ziemlich verrückte Leseerfahrung, denn ich erinnere mich, dass er einen sehr präzisen und technischen Umgang des Wortschatzes in Bezug auf das Meer pflegte und die Gedichte zugleich gefüllt mit erfundenen Wörtern waren. Das Geniale daran war, dass man in vielen dieser Fälle nicht genau zwischen den echten und erfundenen Wörtern unterscheiden konnte. Die erfundenen schienen echt und die echten erfunden. Man spekulierte, und zum Schluss war die Unterscheidung hinfällig. In beiden Fällen benannte man etwas, das ganz klar auf der Welt existierte. Es fehlte nur die Bezeichnung.

Und jetzt, wo ich das lese, denke ich daran, was bei den Wörtern *racha* und *aguaje* vor sich geht. Diese tragen so spezifische Bedeutungen in unserem Jargon, aber hier erscheinen sie in einem Kontext von Gedichten, die versuchen, dieses große mythologische Objekt in seiner ständigen Transformation festzuhalten: der/die? MEER. Was passiert mit der Sprache so nah am Meer? Das Meer bewirkt, dass die Sprache sich lockert und das Ihre macht. Ich denke an Virginia Woolfs Roman *The Waves* und an Martín Adán. Wenn ich *racha* und *aguaje* lese, spüre ich neben dem Jargon (*mala racha*: Pechsträhne; *aguaje*: Lüge) die Koexistenz von anderen Bedeutungen, vielleicht sogar näher am Lyrischen dran. Ich wusste nicht, dass *racha* auch ein Windstoß sein kann. Und *aguaje* mindestens 15 Definitionen im Wörterbuch hat, acht dieser haben einen Zusammenhang zum Meer. Ist das Produkt eine Mischung aus dem Heiligen und Sakrilegischen? Das Meer endet nicht, wie eine Pechsträhne dies tut. Die Darstellung des Meeres wie eine ewige Lüge …

Hallo Claudia,

in Bezug auf den Aliasnamen meiner Kindheit war etwas immer fundamental in meiner Herkunftsgeschichte oder eher fragwürdigen persönlichen Mythologie, meine Eltern gaben mir, bis ich drei Jahre alt war, keinen Namen und ließen mich auch nicht ins Register eintragen. Der Brief meines Vaters ans Meldeamt ist legendär, eine falsche Entschuldigung, begleitet von einer Postanweisung von 1$ als Strafe für die Verzögerung. Dies hat mir über diesen passiven Widerstand geholfen und a priori vom Schicksal befreit zu denken. Ich frage mich, ob der Eigenname als leere Stelle fungieren kann, ein *point de capiton* (Stepppunkt), diese Stellen, an welchen sich das Imaginäre und das Symbolische verweben. Da ich verliebt bin in die Idee der Leere und der Unordnung, liebe ich die Idee, keinen Namen zu haben – wirklich.

Mir gefällt, was Julia Kristeva in diesem Clip[2] über die Echolalie, die erfundenen Wörter, die Musikalität und Kofferwörter sagt. Sie setzt es in Zusammenhang mit dem Präödipalen, dem Mütterlichen – und auch dem Revolutionären.

Als mein Sohn vier oder fünf Jahre alt war, mit seiner älteren Schwester spielte und die Spielbedingungen ändern wollte, wenn die Plastikfigur des Spider-Man auf einmal einen Bäcker darstellen sollte, bat er seine Schwester, das Wort „Bäcker“ so oft zu wiederholen, bis er zufrieden war mit dem Identitätswechsel. Danach wurde das Spiel fortgesetzt. In anderen Momenten mussten weitere Änderungen vorgenommen werden, vielleicht klimatische: Hagel, Hagel, Hagel. In diesem Moment dachte ich mir, dass die Sprache wie Geld ist, man hält sie im Umlauf, sie erhält ihren Wert nur durchs Sprechen – durch Wiederholung, eine gemeinschaftliche Hingabe schaffend. Je banaler, desto besser gelingt es, den Wert des Wortes konstant zu halten.

Bis zu einem gewissen Punkt. Wenn ich an das Gedicht von Pizarnik denke, könnte es sogar das Gegenteil sein, die Abwesenheit. Hagel Hagel Hagel.

Jetzt, mit seinen 17 Jahren, liest er am liebsten *Poemas y antipoemas* von Nicanor Parra. Und wenn er von der Schule kommt und reden möchte, führt das Gespräch ausnahmslos zu den Regeln der Poesie, wie frei der freie Vers ist und das Verhältnis zwischen dem Ästhetischen und Politischen. Auf der anderen Seite steht der Unsinn. Großes Wort, weitreichende Möglichkeiten, beispielsweise in einem Mini-Essay von José Carlos Mariátegui, *In Verteidigung des puren Unsinns.*

> Der pure Unsinn bescheinigt den Tod des bürgerlichen Absoluten. Er prangert den Verfall eines Geistes, einer Philosophie und nicht einer Technik an.
>
> – Veröffentlicht in *Amauta*, N.º 13.
> Geschrieben von José Carlos Mariátegui, 1928

Das führt zu einem ähnlichen Ort wie von Kristeva beschrieben, der Unsinn als Ankündigung und revolutionärer Schriftzug, Tod des bürgerlichen Absoluten. Ich liebe den Unsinn, aber ich mache mir keine Illusionen mehr über den Tod. Ich schreibe dem Unsinn zwar noch immer transformative Fähigkeiten zu, jedoch aus einem anderen Register.

Führen wir unseren Briefwechsel fort?

Hallo Bea,

entschuldige die verspätete Antwort. Gerade muss ich für meine bezahlte Arbeit viel Unsinn korrigieren, den ich in Wahrheit nicht korrigieren möchte … Ich würde auch hier gern den Unsinn verteidigen, aber man lässt mich nicht.

Deine Nachricht bringt mich zurück zu Martín Adán, von dem ich vor einigen Jahren ein wenig besessen war. Als ich in Peru war, entdeckte ich eine Erstausgabe seines *Diario de poeta*. Das hat niemand! Nicht mal meine peruanischen Freunde. Jetzt befindet sich das Buch in einem der Bücherstapel, die sich noch immer seit dem Umzug in meiner Wohnung häufen.

Ich weiß nicht, auf welchen Teil Adáns Arbeit sich Mariátegui bezieht, aber *Travesía de extramares* muss dabei sein. Das Verwunderliche an diesen Gedichten ist die Mischung von Tradition und Avantgarde. Die erste Gedichtsammlung wurde 1950 veröffentlicht, als die Avantgarde in ihrer Hochblüte war. Vallejo und Neruda hatten schon längst ihre Meisterwerke publiziert, *Trilce* und *Residencia en la tierra* (Aufenthalt auf Erden).

Warum entscheidet sich Adán in den 50er-Jahren ein Buch mit Sonetten herauszugeben, voll mit Rubriken (so ähnlich wie das *Passagen-Werk* von Benjamin), wer weiß das schon. Das Buch zählt zu Adáns weniger bekannten, wahrscheinlich deshalb, weil es am nächsten an den Unsinn kommt. Gedichte sind sehr anstrengend zu lesen, denn die aneinandergereihten Wörter ergeben nur schwer Sinn. Zudem sind die Klänge, die Versbrüche, die Rhythmen unangenehm, sie schaffen Dissonanzen. Aber daran zu denken, dass Adán diese Sonette mit der peruanischen Küste vor sich und den Klängen von Chopins *Nocturnes* lauschend schrieb, sagt viel aus, auch wenn ich nicht genau weiß, was. Er gibt die Tradition nicht auf, aber er verändert sie auf eine komische Art und Weise, bis sie sich im Lärm und Unsinn einfindet. Ich denke, es gibt tatsächliche viele Parallelen zu Matos Paoli.

Hier findest Du einige Gedichte, falls Du nicht verstehen, sondern eine Weile lauschen willst:[3]

Machen wir weiter mit unseren Episteeeln,
Claudia

Claudia,

danke für die Zusendung von Martín Adán.

Ich bin bei dem Gedicht mit den erwähnten Ruderschlägen des Charon hängen geblieben, um nicht zu verstehen, warum mich schon seit einigen Wochen das andere beschäftigt, welches sich auf Charon beruft mit "dos veces victorioso crucé el Aqueronte" – und den ich nur durch Kristeva kenne! Das letzte Gedicht von Nerval, *El desdichado* (Du hast mir gerade erst per Nachricht mitgeteilt, dass es Dich an Maelos[4] *El incomprendido* erinnert!), kommt mir vor, entstand vor seinem Suizid, nach dem Tod seiner Liebhaberin. Kristeva orientiert sich in *Schwarze Sonne*, ihrem Buch über Depression und Melancholie, stark an diesem Gedicht.

Die neuen Wörter – unvergänglich? – und dieses *Paire en faceta*, werden wir bei „ein Paar“ sein?

Aus dem Spanischen übersetzt von Elisabeth Gangl

108

1 *Jitanjáfora* ist ein poetisches Stilmittel in der karibischen Poesie, das auf einer spielerischen und rhythmischen Nutzung der Sprache basiert und in der Geschichte und Kultur der afrikanischen Diaspora in der Karibik verwurzelt ist.

2 www.youtube.com/watch?v=tNkLlxzZTys (19. November 2024)

3 www.materialdelectura.unam.mx/poesia-moderna/16-poesia-moderna-cat/279-129-martin-adan?start=3 (19. November 2024)

4 Maelo war der Spitzname von Ismael Rivera (1931–1987), einem puerto-ricanischen Salsa-Sänger.

Beatriz Santiago Muñoz is an artist whose expanded moving image work is entangled with Boalian theater, expanded cinema and feminist practices. She tends to work with non-actors, and incorporates improvisation into her process. Her recent work is on the sensorial unconscious of anti-colonial movements and language experiments. She lives in San Juan. Recent solo exhibitions include: *Ottilia* at Crac-Alsace, *Oriana* in PIVO, Sao Paulo, and argos in Brussels.

Beatriz Santiago Muñoz es una artista cuyo trabajo de cine expandido en movimiento se entrelaza con el teatro boaliano y las prácticas feministas. Tiende a trabajar con actores naturales e incorpora la improvisación en su proceso. Su trabajo reciente se centra en el inconsciente sensorial de los movimientos anticoloniales y los experimentos lingüísticos. Vive en San Juan. Entre sus últimas exposiciones individuales se incluyen: *Ottilia* en Crac-Alsace, *Oriana* en PIVO, Sao Paulo, y argos en Bruselas.

Beatriz Santiago Muñoz ist eine Künstlerin, deren erweiterte Bewegtbildarbeit mit dem Boal'schen Theater, Expanded Cinema und feministischen Praktiken verwoben ist. Sie arbeitet bevorzugt mit Amateurschauspieler*innen und bezieht Improvisation in ihre Prozesse mit ein. In ihren jüngsten Arbeiten beschäftigt sie sich mit dem sensorischen Unbewussten der antikolonialen Bewegungen und mit Sprachexperimenten. Sie lebt in San Juan, Puerto Rico. Zu ihren jüngsten Einzelausstellungen gehören *Ottilia* im CRAC Alsace und *Oriana* im Pivô, São Paulo, sowie im argos, Brüssel.

110

Claudia Becerra is a writer and teacher from Puerto Rico. She has published two poetry collections: *Versión del viaje* (Folium, 2018) and *Sirenas* (Riel, 2023). Her work has appeared in various journals and magazines, among these *La pequeña, Rialta, Lucerna, América Invertida, Distrópika, Cruce, Institute of Caribbean Studies, Words Without Borders*, and *Claridad*. Between 2018–2022 she coedited *The Puerto Rico Review*. Becerra holds a BA degree from the University of Puerto Rico, Río Piedras Campus, and a PhD in Latin American Poetry from Brown University. She currently teaches at the University of Vermont.

Claudia Becerra escribe y enseña. Ha publicado dos poemarios: *Versión del viaje* (Folium, 2018) y *Sirenas* (Riel, 2023). Su trabajo ha figurado en diversos medios puertorriqueños (y del más allá), entre ellos, *La pequeña, Rialta, Lucerna, América Invertida, Distrópika, Cruce, Caribbean Studies Journal* y el periódico *Claridad*. Entre 2018–2022 coeditó la revista *The Puerto Rico Review*. Tiene un bachillerato de la Universidad de Puerto Rico, Recinto de Río Piedras, y un doctorado en poesía latinoamericana de Brown University. Actualmente enseña en la Universidad de Vermont.

Claudia Becerra ist eine Schriftstellerin und Professorin aus Puerto Rico. Sie hat zwei Gedichtbände veröffentlicht: *Versión del viaje* (Folium, 2018) und *Sirenas* (Riel, 2023). Ihre Arbeiten sind in verschiedenen Zeitschriften und Magazinen erschienen, darunter *La pequeña, Rialta, Lucerna, América Invertida, Distrópika, Cruce, Institute of Caribbean Studies, Words Without Borders* und *Claridad*. Von 2018–2022 war sie Mitherausgeberin von *The Puerto Rico Review*. Becerra hat einen BA-Abschluss von der Universidad de Puerto Rico, Río Piedras Campus, und einen Doktortitel in lateinamerikanischer Poesie von der Brown University. Derzeit lehrt sie an der University of Vermont.

This book is published on the occasion of the exhibition Beatriz Santiago Muñoz. *Elogio al disparate* at the Secession, December 6, 2024–February 23, 2025.

Publisher:
Secession
Editor:
Bettina Spörr
Publication manager:
Tina Lipsky
Series design concept:
Sabo Day
Graphic design:
Rosen Eveleigh
Photo credit:
Beatriz Santiago Muñoz
Texts:
Claudia Beccera
Beatriz Santiago Muñoz
Translations:
Nicole C. Delgado Poueymirou
Elisabeth Gangl
Copyediting and proofreading:
Charlotte Eckler
Martin Gastl (m∞bius)
Nicole C. Delgado Poueymirou
Printed and produced by:
Medienfabrik Graz
Print run:
400

Intervention by the artist:
This small publication contains a selection literary texts and extracts, mostly poetry, related to the *jitanjáfora* and nonsense poetry, as well as to the quasi magical and contradictory qualities of the word which can invoke or make invisible, destroy or create. The horizontal slide into the nonsense word, so often used by Caribbean speakers, poets and singers opens up a hole in language into the non-existent and not yet named.

Verlag der Buchhandlung
Walther und Franz König
Ehrenstraße 4
D–50672 Köln

Distribution:
Buchhandlung Walther König
Ehrenstraße 4
D–50672 Köln
Tel: +49 (0) 221/20 59 6 53
verlag@buchhandlung-walther-koenig.de

ISBN 978-3-7533-0630-8

Printed in the EU

Secession

Exhibition
Beatriz Santiago Muñoz. *Elogio al Disparate*

Curator:
Bettina Spörr
Installation crew:
Miriam Bachmann
Hans Weinberger
Andrei Galtsov
with Said Gärtner
Tristan Griessler
Wolfgang Lehninger
Alex Pasch
Christian Rasser
Sebastian Scholz
Johanna Steiner
Lorenz Sutter
Kai Trausenegger
Marton Zalka

The exhibition programme is conceived by the Board of the Secession.

Board of the Association of Visual Artists Secession

President:
Ramesch Daha
Vice-presidents:
Barbara Kapusta
Jun Yang
Secretary:
Michael Part
Treasurer:
Axel Stockburger
Members:
Ricarda Denzer
Philipp Fleischmann
Wilfried Kühn
Ulrike Müller
Nick Oberthaler
Lisl Ponger
Sophie Thun
Anna Witt
Jun Yang

Auditors:
Thomas Baumann
Susi Jirkuff
Management:
Magdalena Ritter
Curators:
Damian Lentini
Jeanette Pacher
Bettina Spörr
Gallery managers:
Miriam Bachmann
Hans Weinberger
Facility manager, audiovisual engineering:
Andrei Galtsov
Publication manager:
Tina Lipsky
Head of Partnership Development:
Nina Buchwaldt
Public relations:
Romana Heinlein
Julia Kronberger (on educational leave)
Marketing:
Zuzanna Zajac
Visual concept, graphic design Secession:
Sabo Day
Archive:
Tina Lipsky
Hessam Samavatian
Art education coordination:
Katharina Schniebs
Art education:
Paul Buschnegg,
Grzegorz Kielawski
Cristina Rüesch
Accounting:
Beatrix Münzberger
Shop management:
Gabriele Grabler
Assistant to the management:
Kathrin Schweizer
Administrative assistant:
Albert Warpechowski

Visitor service:
Mario Heuschober
Niklas Hofstetter
Anita Husar
Fiona Idahosa
Liana Isakhanyan
Nakale Lefaza-Botowamungu
Gloria Linares-Higueras
Carmen Linares de Schubert
Florian Moser
Sabine Schlemmel
Wei Ling Zheng
Cleaners:
Emine Koza
& Firma Simacek
Web design:
Treat Agency

The Board of the Secession would like to thank the Secession Friends for supporting the project with their research.

Patrons of the Secession Friends

Sandra Bär Heuer
Martin Böhm – Dorotheum
Susanne Breiner Wojnar
KR Anton Feistl
Roman & Margot Fuchs – Sammlung Fuchs
Dr. Burkhard & Gabriela Gantenbein
Dr. Christian Hauer
Franziska & Christian Hausmaninger
Felicitas Hausner
Alexander Kahane
Louis & Mafalda Kahane
Dr. Christoph & Bernadette Kraus – Kraus & Kraus Family Office
Franz Krummel & Mira Kloss-Zechner
Péter Küllői
Ronald & Jo Carole Lauder
Dr. Robert & Sylvie Liska
Maria Lassnig Foundation
Hema Makwana & Felix Wolfmair
Barbara Mechtler-Habig & Roland Mechtler
Dr. Arend & Brigitte Oetker
Galerie Thaddaeus Ropac
Franz Seilern
Stefan Stolitzka – SLE Schuh GmbH
Stefan & Elisabeth Weber
Wiener Städtische Versicherungsverein
Otto Ernst Wiesenthal – Hotel Altstadt Vienna
Katharina Wruss

Esta pequeña publicación contiene una selección de textos y extractos literarios, en su mayoría poesía, relacionados con la jitanjáfora y la poesía sin sentido, así como con las cualidades casi mágicas y contradictorias de la palabra que puede invocar o invisibilizar, destruir o crear. El deslizamiento horizontal hacia la palabra sin sentido, tan frecuentemente utilizada por hablantes, poetas y cantantes caribeños, abre un agujero en el lenguaje hacia lo inexistente y aún no nombrado.

Main Sponsor

ERSTE

Stadt Wien Kultur

Bundesministerium Kunst, Kultur, öffentlicher Dienst und Sport

secession friends

secession
Vereinigung bildender Künstler*innen Wiener Secession
Friedrichstraße 12
1010 Vienna
www.secession.at